D1315437

EXPLORING OUR SOLAR SYSTEM

THE EARTH

DAVID JEFFERIS

Crabtree

■ ABOUT THE EARTH

The Earth is our home in space, one of eight major planets that circle the Sun. Our world is not the smallest planet, or the biggest, but it is very special. The Earth is the only place in the universe where we know for certain that life exists.

Scientific evidence suggests that the Earth formed about 4.6 billion years ago, and that life began on Earth within a billion years after that. Exactly how this happened we do not know. Since then, living things have filled Earth's seas, air, and the land, from **pole** to pole.

Crabtree Publishing Company
PMB 16A,
350 Fifth Avenue, Suite 3308
New York, NY 10118

616 Welland Avenue,
St. Catharines, Ontario
L2M 5V6

Editors: Ellen Rodger,
Adrianna Morganelli

Published by Crabtree Publishing Company © 2008

Written and produced by:
David Jefferis/Buzz Books

Educational advisor:
Julie Stapleton

Science advisor:
Mat Irvine FBIS

■ ACKNOWLEDGEMENTS

We wish to thank all those people who have helped to create this publication. Information and images were supplied by:

Agencies and organizations:
  ESA European Space Agency
  JAMSTEC Japan Marine-Earth Science
  JPL Jet Propulsion Laboratory
  NASA Space Agency
  NOAA Oceanic and Atmospheric Agency
  NSF National Science Foundation
  OPP Office of Polar Programs
  Wikimedia
Collections:
  Alpha Archive
  iStockphoto:
    Trevor Bauer
    Jodie Coston
    Roman Krochuk
    Veronique Le Velly
    Jason Maehl
    James Steidl
Individuals:
  Tony Bostrom
  Nicolle Rager-Fuller/NSF

Cross-section of the Earth based on a diagram by Calvin J. Hamilton

Library and Archives Canada Cataloguing in Publication

Jefferis, David   The earth : our home planet / David Jefferis.

(Exploring our solar system) Includes index.
ISBN 978-0-7787-3730-8 (bound).--
ISBN 978-0-7787-3746-9 (pbk.)

      1. Earth--Juvenile literature. I. Title. II. Series: Exploring our solar system (St. Catharines, Ont.)

QB631.4.J43 2008   j525   C2008-901517-7

Library of Congress Cataloging-in-Publication Data

Jefferis, David.
  The Earth : our home planet / David Jefferis.
      p. cm. -- (Exploring our solar system)
  Includes index.
  ISBN-13: 978-0-7787-3746-9 (pbk. : alk. paper)
  ISBN-10: 0-7787-3746-2 (pbk. : alk. paper)
  ISBN-13: 978-0-7787-3730-8 (reinforced library binding : alk. paper)
  ISBN-10: 0-7787-3730-6 (reinforced library binding : alk. paper)
  1. Earth--Juvenile literature. I. Title.
  QB631.4.J44 2008
  525--dc22
                                        2008008778

■CONTENTS

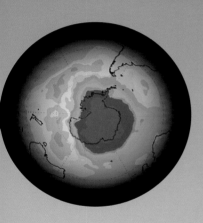

■ WHAT IS THE EARTH?

The Earth is one of eight major planets that circle around the Sun. It is a sphere that is 7,927 miles (12,756 km) across.

■ The planets to scale. Left to right, they are: Mercury, Venus, Earth, Mars, Jupiter, Saturn, Uranus, and Neptune.

Earth is the "third rock" from the Sun

■ IS THE EARTH A BIG PLANET?

Compared with giant planets like Jupiter and Saturn, the Earth is small. It is the biggest of the four planets nearest to the Sun – Mercury, Venus, Earth, and Mars. These planets all have rocky surfaces. The four outer planets may be huge, but they are simply balls of gas.

■ The Earth and Moon are often called a "double planet." Most moons are far smaller compared to the size of their parent planet.

The Moon is 2,160 miles (3,476 km) across.

The Earth is 7,927 miles (12,756 km) across.

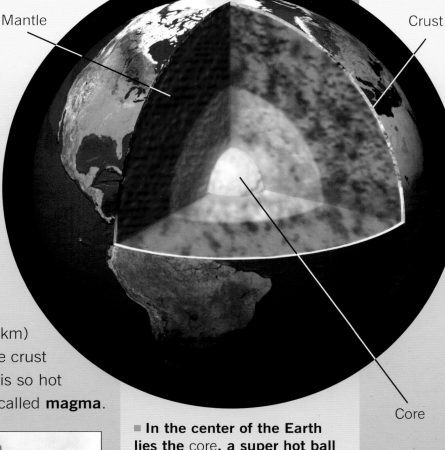

Mantle

Crust

Core

■ IS THE EARTH A SOLID BALL OF ROCK?

The Earth is far from a ball of rock. The only solid parts are the surface rocks of the Earth's **crust**. Compared to the size of the Earth, the crust is barely as thick as an orange peel . It varies from just four miles (six km) thick under the oceans, to about 20 to 30 miles (30 to 50 km) on the continents. Just below the crust is the outer **mantle**. The mantle is so hot that the rock is a searing **mass**, called **magma**.

■ In the center of the Earth lies the core, **a super hot ball thought to be made mostly of iron. Outside this is the mantle, also very hot. The outer mantle, on which the crust floats, is thick. It flows much like hot, sticky syrup.**

■ IS THE EARTH A VERY UNUSUAL PLANET?

It certainly is! The Earth is the only planet we know of that is just the right temperature for water to exist in its three forms – gas in the air, liquid in lakes, rivers, and seas, and solid ice in cold regions. This allows our planet to support life, which needs water to survive.

WOW!
The Earth is sometimes called a "Goldilocks" planet, after the fairytale. The Earth is not too hot, not too cold, but is "just right" for living things.

■ HOW OLD IS THE EARTH?

The latest theories say the Earth is about 4.6 billion years old. Scientists think it formed from a large, slowly turning, dust cloud in space.

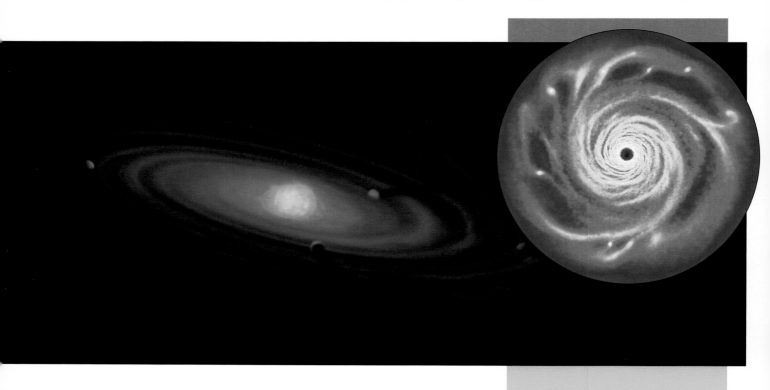

■ HOW QUICKLY DID THE EARTH FORM?

We do not know exactly, but studies have shown that it could have taken only a few million years for a gassy cloud of dust and rock to form both the Sun and the planets. It is a process astronomers say is taking place today, in gas clouds far away in space.

■ These pictures show how the Sun and planets might have looked billions of years ago. The view above is a computer simulation, with planets forming, like clots of cream in a cup of coffee.

WOW!
The early Earth was probably hit by an object about the size of the planet Mars. Material was "splashed off" into space to eventually form the Moon.

■ WHEN DID LIFE APPEAR ON THE YOUNG EARTH?

Scientists think the first living things, which were no more than very simple **organisms**, appeared about a billion years after Earth formed. Life could have resulted from a mixture of just the right materials. These materials may have even rained down from space. No one knows the answer yet. There are only ideas and theories so far.

■ HAS THE EARTH CHANGED SINCE ITS FORMATION?

Yes it has! Early changes included cooling down from a fiery birth. The **atmosphere** and oceans also altered the face of the planet. The Earth is still changing today, because the continents are not stationary. Instead, the landmasses float on the mantle, and drift slowly, at about 1.5 inches (38 mm) a year.

■ These globes show how scientists think the continents have drifted in the past. It is a process called continental drift, in which giant "plates" of rock move slowly around the world. Sometimes they split apart, other times they join together.

1 275 million years ago.
2 220 million years ago.
3 150 million years ago.
4 100 million years ago.
5 Present day.

1

2

3

4

5

■ The Earth's surface is also being changed constantly by weather, wind, and waves.

■ WHAT WILL HAPPEN IN THE FUTURE?

The continents will continue to drift, and the familiar look of today's globe will one day be very different. But it is a slow process, and things will look much the same for the next few million years.

■ HOW DOES THE EARTH MOVE IN SPACE?

The Earth turns on its axis to give us night and day. It also travels around the Sun, circling it completely once a year.

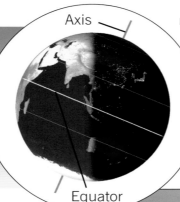

Axis

Equator

□ **The Earth turns once every 24 hours. Day and night are roughly 12 hours each in most parts of the world. At the poles, days and nights last for months at a time.**

■ WHAT IS THE EARTH'S AXIS?

The axis is an invisible line between the North and South poles, around which the Earth rotates. The Earth's axis lies at an angle, 23.5 degrees from vertical. This is called the axial tilt.

■ WHAT IS A YEAR?

A **year** is the time it takes to complete an **orbit**, the near-circular path the Earth takes around the Sun. The distance does vary a little. It averages 93 million miles (150 million km), with near and far points called the perihelion and the **aphelion**.

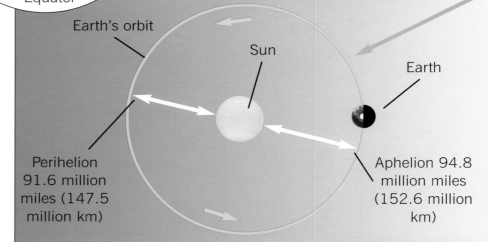

Earth's orbit

Sun

Earth

Perihelion 91.6 million miles (147.5 million km)

Aphelion 94.8 million miles (152.6 million km)

WOW!
The Earth moves at a good speed in its orbit around the Sun. Every hour, our planet travels about 67,000 miles (108,000 km) through space!

■ DO WE HAVE WINTER AT APHELION?

No. Distance from the Sun does not affect the seasons. The Earth's axial tilt does, because different parts of the world receive more or less light (and warmth) as the year progresses. Also, it means that the Earth's northern and southern hemispheres have opposite seasons. Summer in the north is winter in the south.

■ **Earth's circular orbit is not quite a true circle, making us a little nearer or further away from the Sun as we move around it.**

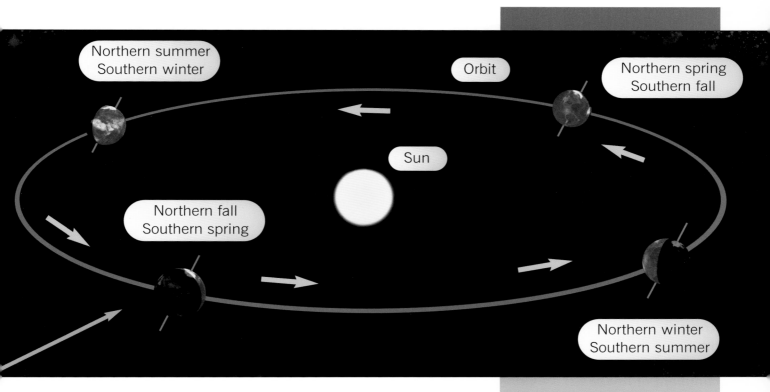

Northern summer
Southern winter

Orbit

Northern spring
Southern fall

Sun

Northern fall
Southern spring

Northern winter
Southern summer

■ SO WHAT MAKES THE SEASONS?

In much of the world the year is divided into four seasons. In June, the northern half of the Earth leans toward the Sun and receives more sunlight than the south. In December, the opposite is true. In April and September, things are balanced evenly. These mark the mid-points of spring and fall.

■ WHAT ABOUT OTHER PLACES?

The tropical parts of planet Earth – those that are at or near the **equator** – have much less seasonal changes, because they receive strong sunshine all year round.

■ These globes mark four points in the Earth's orbital path around the Sun, called the solstices (winter and summer), and the equinoxes (spring and fall).

They are the mid-points of each season. For example, the winter solstice is when the Sun appears lowest in the northern sky. At the same moment in southern skies, the Sun appears at its highest point.

■ The seasons bring a different face to many parts of the world as a year progresses. In spring, plants bud and grow, maturing during summer. In fall, leaves fall before the snows of winter.

9 ■

■ WHERE ARE THE DEEP FREEZE ZONES?

The Earth's tilted axis means that the North and South poles are in near-darkness for months at a time, making them frozen, icy wastelands.

■ The polar regions are both cold, but the ice around the North Pole floats in the Arctic Ocean. Ice at the South Pole lies mostly on land on the continent of Antarctica.

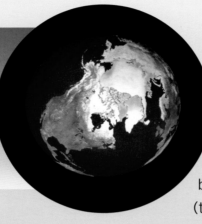

■ WHERE IS THE NORTH POLE?

The North Pole is not on land at all. It is in the middle of the 13,000 ft (4,000 m) deep Arctic Ocean. Polar ice floats in the water and is always shifting around, so a permanent research station cannot be built. The ice is often less than ten feet (three meters) thick.

WOW!
In 2005, a U.S. submarine punched its way up through five ft (1.5 m) of ice at the North Pole. It spent 18 hours there, before diving again.

■ HOW COLD IS THE NORTH POLE?

With winter temperatures down to about -45°F (-43°C), the North Pole is icy cold. It is much warmer than the South Pole. This is mostly because the Arctic waters soak up the Sun's summer heat, releasing it slowly in winter.

■ The Arctic is not a silent place. The ice constantly "growls" as it moves around in the water.

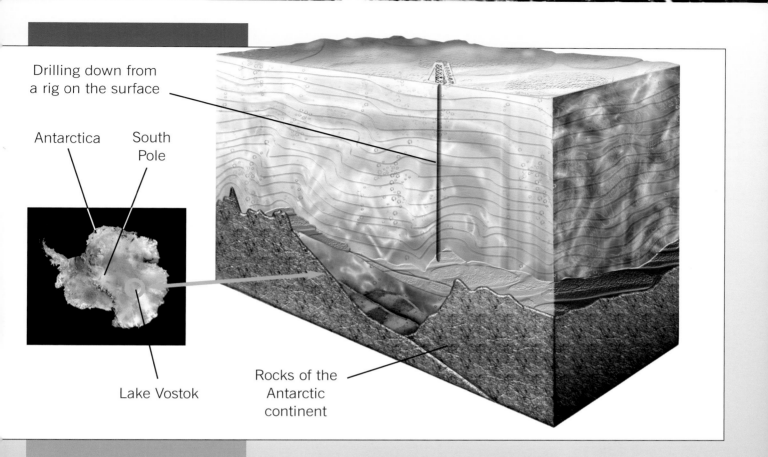

Drilling down from a rig on the surface

Antarctica

South Pole

Lake Vostok

Rocks of the Antarctic continent

■ Lake Vostok is buried deep under the ice of Antarctica. It is the deepest under-ice lake in the world, lying about 2.5 miles (4 km) below the frozen surface.

■ WHAT IS THE VOSTOK STATION?

It is a research base in Antarctica, set up in 1957. It is run by scientists of countries such as France, Russia, and the U.S. Vostok holds the record for being the Earth's coldest place—in 1983 the temperature sank to a chilly -128.6°F (-89.2°C). Even in mid-summer, it is no warmer than -2°F (-19°C).

■ AND WHAT ABOUT PLANET EARTH'S HOT ZONES?

These are the hot **deserts**, the biggest of which is the Sahara Desert, in North Africa. The Sahara covers an area nearly as big as the U.S. It is not just sandy desert. Much of it is covered in bare rocks. Temperatures can be hot enough to fry an egg. The highest temperature recorded there was 136°F (57.8°C).

■ Deserts are not all covered with sand and palm trees. Antarctica is also considered a desert, because it is very dry there. Deserts are arid places.

WHAT IS INSIDE THE EARTH?

The Earth's interior is filled with molten rock. The solid rocks of the continents float like giant crackers in a bowl of thick, super hot soup.

WHY DOES A VOLCANO ERUPT?

A **volcano** links the hot mantle and the surface. Scorching hot magma blasts into the air through a crack or fissure in the crust. The magma cools to form lava. Lava often flows in a burning river of fire until it cools off enough to form solid rock.

Volcanoes can spew huge amounts of deadly gases, smoke, and dust. These, plus tremors and earthquakes, **may turn big eruptions into deadly killers.**

The worst such volcano was on Krakatoa, in Indonesia. In 1883, it exploded, killing more than 36,000 people, and wiping out nearly 300 towns and villages.

The explosions were heard up to 3,000 miles (5,000 km) away!

WOW!
The worst tsunami on record was in 2004, when more than 230,000 people were killed in coastal areas around the Pacific and Indian oceans.

WHAT IS A TSUNAMI?

A **tsunami** is a tidal wave caused by the shocks from an underwater earthquake. Tsunamis can be destructive and deadly.

■ The "Ring of Fire" (arrows) is a zone that circles the Pacific Ocean, where various plates bump into each other.

WHAT ARE PLATE TECTONICS?

This is the name for the way that the Earth's crust is broken up into a dozen or so plates. Plates are giant continents of solid rock that move slowly as they ride on top of the much hotter mantle. The continents move very slowly, at about the same rate as your fingernails grow.

■ The mountains of Pakistan are another earthquake zone. Here, a survivor from a 2006 'quake stands next to his wrecked home. The blue tent behind him belongs to an international rescue team.

WHAT IS A SUBDUCTION ZONE?

This is where two plates collide. One sinks slowly under the other, into the mantle. The Earth is the only planet where **subduction** happens. The other rocky planets, and the Moon, are "dead" so far as any plate movements are concerned.

■ Here an ocean plate grinds against a continental plate. Ocean plates are thinner, so they usually sink into the mantle.

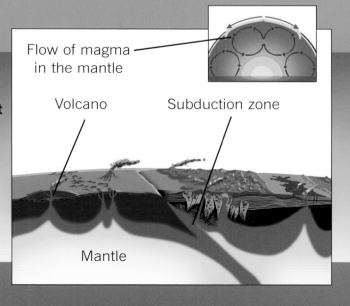

Flow of magma in the mantle

Volcano

Subduction zone

Mantle

HOW ARE MOUNTAINS FORMED?

When the continental plates bump into each other, their edges buckle and heave, creating new mountain ranges.

■ The Himalayan mountain range was formed by the Indian plate's northward path. Where the Indian and Asian plates grind together, their edges buckle upward.

■ HOW FAST DO MOUNTAINS GROW?

It is not a quick process, and depends on how fast plates are bumping into each other. The highest peaks in the Asian Himalaya range grow about a half-inch (1.2 cm) taller each year. Scientists can check the height by using sensitive measuring equipment aboard **satellites** orbiting the Earth.

■ WHAT IS THE HIGHEST MOUNTAIN?

At first sight, Earth's highest peak looks like a volcanic island in the Pacific Ocean. But the "island" is actually the summit of the underwater mountain Mauna Kea, in Hawaii. It rises all the way from the deep ocean floor to an overall height of 33,465 ft (10,200 m). Less than one-third of this is above sea level.

■ WHAT IS A SEAMOUNT?

A **seamount** is an undersea mountain whose top does not reach the surface. Seamounts are mostly volcanic, formed by scorching hot lava that pours out of cracks in the crust. There are probably about 30,000 seamounts. Some are uncharted. In 2005, a U.S. submarine nearly sank when it crashed at full speed into an unknown seamount in the Pacific Ocean!

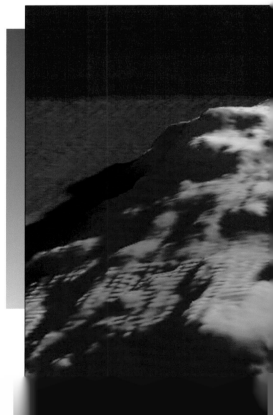

■ WHAT IS THE HIGHEST LAND MOUNTAIN?

The world's highest land mountain is Mount Everest, in the Himalayas. It is 29,028 ft (8,848 m) high, depending on the amount of snow on top. Plate movements are constantly shifting the Himalayas. Everest grows upward and sideways at just half a fingernail-length each year. Some researchers also say it is shrinking!

WOW!
Everest is a forbidding place, but there is some life up there. Spiders live in rock cracks, and geese have been seen flying not far from the top.

□ No one managed to climb Mt Everest until 1953. Today, it is a popular, if not dangerous, site for climbers. Over the years, more than 200 people have died trying to reach the mountain's top.

■ This computer image shows a seamount rising from the Pacific Ocean floor.

You can see that it is volcanic by the circular crater, or caldera, at the top. Bubbling lava has poured out of this, slowly building this undersea mountain as it cools off.

Sometimes a seamount may collapse. The shocks from this can trigger a tsunami.

■IS THE EARTH A GIANT MAGNET?

The Earth's iron-rich outer core creates huge electric currents as it swirls slowly under our feet. These currents also produce the Earth's magnetic field.

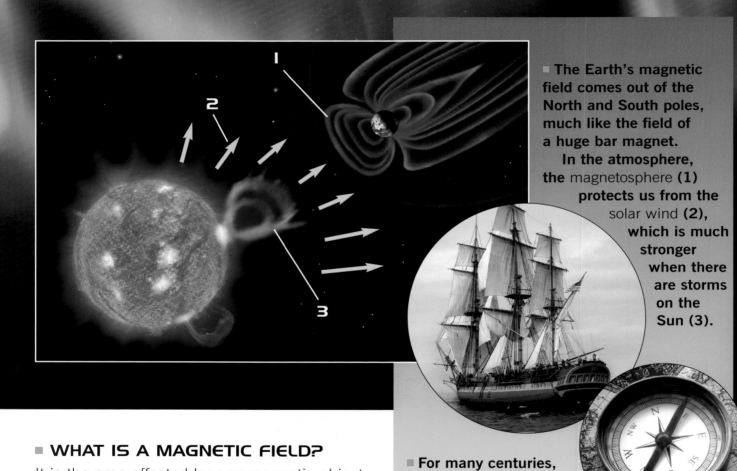

■ The Earth's magnetic field comes out of the North and South poles, much like the field of a huge bar magnet.

In the atmosphere, the magnetosphere **(1)** protects us from the solar wind **(2)**, which is much stronger when there are storms on the Sun **(3)**.

■ WHAT IS A MAGNETIC FIELD?

It is the area affected by any magnetic object, whether it is a small bar magnet or a massive object, such as the Earth.

The Earth is not the only **solar system** object to have a magnetic field. The Sun has a powerful one, as do several planets, including Jupiter, Saturn, Uranus, and Neptune.

■ For many centuries, the Earth's magnetic field has been used by ships' navigators. Using a compass, a route could be charted for even the longest voyages.

It was not until spacecraft started to explore space near the Earth that we knew anything about the invisible magnetic zone that surrounds and protects us.

■ HOW DOES THE MAGNETOSPHERE PROTECT US?

The magnetosphere is the name for the region of space affected by the Earth's magnetic field. It surrounds our world, which is important because it forms a natural shield against the solar wind. Solar winds are tiny, but deadly particles that pour from the Sun. The magnetosphere deflects most of them away from the Earth.

■ Spectacular auroras are a common sight in the night skies of countries near the poles.

■ IS THE SOLAR WIND ALWAYS DANGEROUS?

When the Sun is calm, there is little danger. But the solar wind may suddenly become a storm strong enough to damage electronic equipment on spacecraft, and power lines on the Earth. The same particles can be harmful to humans, causing cancers and other diseases.

■ WHAT ARE AURORAS?

From the ground, **auroras** look like moving curtains of misty light. They appear mostly in polar skies, and are the result of energy given off when the solar wind hits the magnetosphere.

■HOW BIG ARE THE OCEANS?

It is no surprise that the Earth looks like a beautiful blue marble from space. Most of Earth's surface is covered with water.

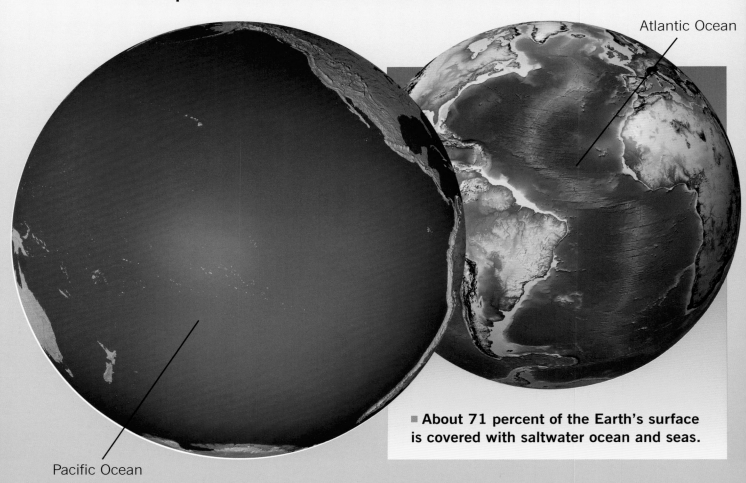

Atlantic Ocean

Pacific Ocean

■ **About 71 percent of the Earth's surface is covered with saltwater ocean and seas.**

WOW!
The saltwater oceans hold almost all the water on our planet. Freshwater, including glaciers, rivers, and lakes, make up just three percent of the total.

■ **WHICH IS THE BIGGEST OCEAN?**
This is the Pacific Ocean, which covers almost half of the planet. The oceans are not really separate at all. Their waters swirl together all across the globe.

■ **Undersea smokers (1) on the ocean floor show where very hot gases leak through the Earth's crust. Strange animals living in the dark depths include many kinds of starfish (2). The *Trieste* (3) made a record dive in 1960.**

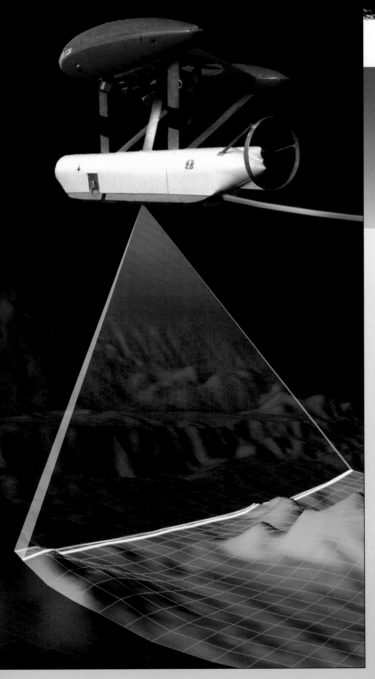

■ Mapping the ocean floor is a job for a Remote Operated Vehicle (ROV). A human operator on the surface controls the ROV by sending commands down a long cable. Information from various scanners on the ROV record the view down below.

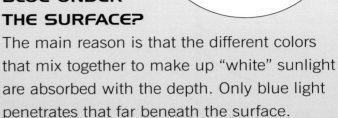

■ WHY DO THINGS LOOK BLUE UNDER THE SURFACE?

The main reason is that the different colors that mix together to make up "white" sunlight are absorbed with the depth. Only blue light penetrates that far beneath the surface.

■ WHICH IS THE DEEPEST OCEAN?

The Pacific Ocean has the deepest point. It is called the Marianas Trench and is in the western Pacific. A trip from the surface to the ocean floor here is a journey 35,838 ft (10,923 m) down. In 1960, two men reached the bottom during a risky exploration mission in a research sub called the *Trieste*.

1

2

3

WHAT IS THE ATMOSPHERE?

The atmosphere is the layer of gases surrounding the Earth. Without the atmosphere, life on Earth would not be possible.

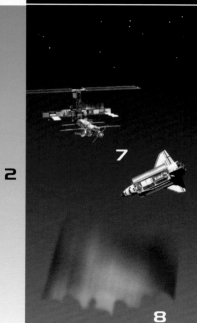

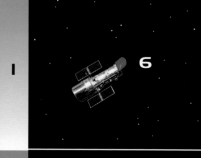

■ **The Earth's air is in layers:**
1 **Exosphere**
2 **Thermosphere**
3 **Mesosphere**
4 **Stratosphere**
5 **Troposphere**

Satellites and many spacecraft (6,7) orbit in the exosphere and thermosphere. The auroras (8) occur high in the atmosphere. Meteors (9) burn up in the mesosphere. Airliners (10) cruise in the stratosphere. Most clouds (11) occur in the troposphere.

■ WHAT GASES MAKE UP THE ATMOSPHERE?

The air is made up mostly of nitrogen (78 percent) and oxygen (21 percent). Argon and carbon dioxide are next, with traces of others forming the rest. Ozone is an important gas, even though there is very little of it. It forms a thin layer more than six miles (ten km) up, which shields us from deadly solar rays.

■ HOW THICK IS THE ATMOSPHERE?

75 percent of the Earth's atmosphere lies below a height of 6.8 miles (11 km), and most weather clouds are in the troposphere, from ground level up to four to ten miles (seven to 17 km). The atmosphere has no upper limit. It just gets thinner, until at 62 miles (100 km) up, there is so little left that it is called "space."

WOW!
Hurricanes are among the most violent storms on Earth. Winds blowing in a powerful hurricane can reach more than 190 mph (306 km/h).

The thickest clouds are shown in red in this satellite map of the Earth

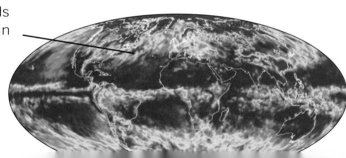

■ WHERE DID THE ATMOSPHERE COME FROM?

The air today is very different to Earth's early days, when thousands of huge volcanoes belched out steam and poison gases. Much of this gassy mix was absorbed by the oceans. Later on, early life forms breathed out oxygen as part of their waste. Plants, especially algae plants in the seas, keep pumping out the oxygen we need to breathe.

■ Clouds are not limited to the Earth's air layers. Six other planets, and some moons, in the solar system have atmospheres with clouds. Their makeup is very different to that of the Earth's air.

1	Jupiter	Upper cloud layers of ammonia.
2	Saturn	Upper cloud layers of ammonia.
3	Uranus	Methane clouds.
4	Neptune	Methane clouds.
5	Earth	Water vapor.
6	Venus	Sulphuric acid droplets.
7	Mars	Thin high clouds of water ice.

IS GLOBAL WARMING A DANGER?

Global warming is a serious problem of an overheating Earth, caused by too many waste gases being released into the atmosphere.

WHY ARE GASES CAUSING A PROBLEM?

Gases in the air, mostly water vapor and carbon dioxide, trap some of the Sun's heat. This is a natural "**greenhouse effect**," and it keeps the world at a comfortable temperature. By burning fossil fuels, humans pollute the atmosphere with large amounts of waste gases, such as carbon dioxide. These add to the natural greenhouse effect, and create the problem called global warming.

WOW!
Greenhouse gases warm the world by 59°F (33°C), making it a comfy place to live. It is human-made waste gases that are the main issue.

WILL THE ICE CAPS MELT?

The ice cap around the North Pole is already melting. Some areas that used to be solid ice all year round are now open water in the summer months.

Our planet is warming up a little too much.

Melting glacial ice in Antarctica and Greenland could raise sea levels, flooding low-lying countries across the world. Disease-carrying mosquitoes could become a danger in places that used to be too cool for them to survive.

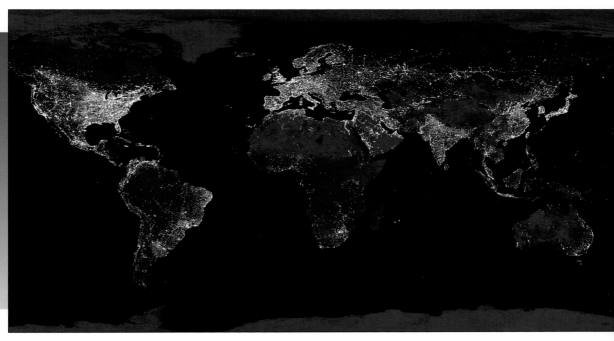

■ The lights of cities at night shows how dependant humans are on fossil fuels. Burning fuels such as oil and coal to power our world seems to be one of the main reasons for global warming.

■ WHAT CAN WE DO TO AVOID DISASTER?

Whatever we do to reduce levels of greenhouse gases, most scientists believe that the world will still heat up a few degrees during the 21st century. Global warming is here already.

We can help to reduce the rise in temperature by replacing old-fashioned oil and coal-burning machines with ones that run cleanly, without harming the environment and adding greenhouse gases. Nuclear, wind, wave, and solar energy are ways to make electricity without producing greenhouse gases.

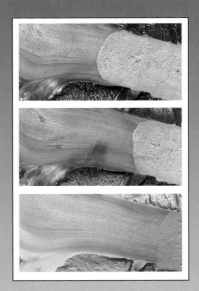

■ The satellite pictures above show how global warming seems to be affecting the world. Here a glacier in Greenland has been photographed over three years. Each year, the glacier shrinks, because the ice has melted more than usual.

WHAT IS THE BIOSPHERE?

A biosphere **is the name for the parts of the Earth that support life, in the lithosphere (land), the** hydrosphere **(water) and the atmosphere (air).**

■ HOW MANY LIVING THINGS ARE THERE ON PLANET EARTH?

There is no exact answer, but about 1.75 million different kinds of plants and animals is the best guess. New animals and species are being discovered all the time, and some researchers think there could be 10 million or more.

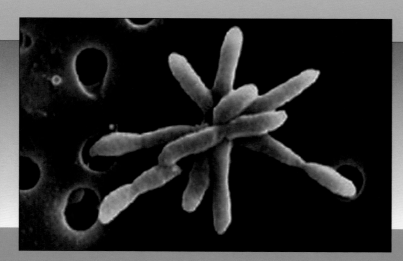

■ **Amazingly, there are huge numbers of tiny organisms living in the rocks deep beneath the Earth's surface.**

Some research shows that the total amount of these "extremophile" life forms could be greater than all the animals and plants living in the biosphere above.

■ WHICH IS THE BIGGEST PLANT?

The biggest individual plant is thought to be a huge tree that grows in California. The trunk of this enormous sequoia tree, called *General Sherman* weighs about 2,000 tons – and that is without including the leaves and branches! The giant tree is almost 275 ft (83.8 m) tall.

■ Giants of the biosphere include the sequoia tree (1) the African elephant (2) and the blue whale (3).

The biosphere is divided into biomes, or zones that support plants and animals that thrive in a similar environment. Biomes near the Arctic and Antarctic are fairly barren, but ones in the world's warmer and wetter zones teem with living things.

■ AND THE BIGGEST ANIMAL?

This is the huge blue whale, which also holds the record for the biggest animal that has ever lived. The largest blue whale ever measured was 110 ft 2 in (33.58 m) long and weighed 210 tons. Land animals are much smaller, because they do not have water to support such a heavy weight. Even so, the biggest land animal is impressive. The male African elephant can weigh more than 12 tons!

WOW!
The bumblebee bat is the smallest non-insect flyer. It grows to just over one inch (30 mm) long. The bee-sized bat lives mostly in Thailand.

■ WHAT ARE EARTH RESOURCES SATELLITES?

Earth Resources Satellites are satellites that study the Earth, instead of gazing far out into the universe. Such satellites send us a constant stream of information on the health of our world.

■ WHAT IS THE WORLD WEATHER LIKE?

It is only since the first weather satellites were fired into orbit in the 1960s that we have been able to get a good idea of the Earth's weather systems. The picture below is a good example of what can be seen from space. It shows all the world's cloud cover in one day.

WOW!
Landsat can take 500-plus pictures each day. It orbits the Earth at a height of about 435 miles (700 km) and can scan the whole planet in just 16 days.

■ CAN SATELLITES STOP GLOBAL WARMING?

Not by themselves, but they do give us an accurate picture, and this is vital to see what is really happening around the world. Satellites are one of the key tools to help us save the planet.

■ The U.S. Landsat 7 is the latest in a line of Earth Resources Satellites that started in 1972. Like many such satellites, Landsat 7 takes a series of pictures as it passes over the world. It can record such things as plant growth, pollution, snow cover, and much more.

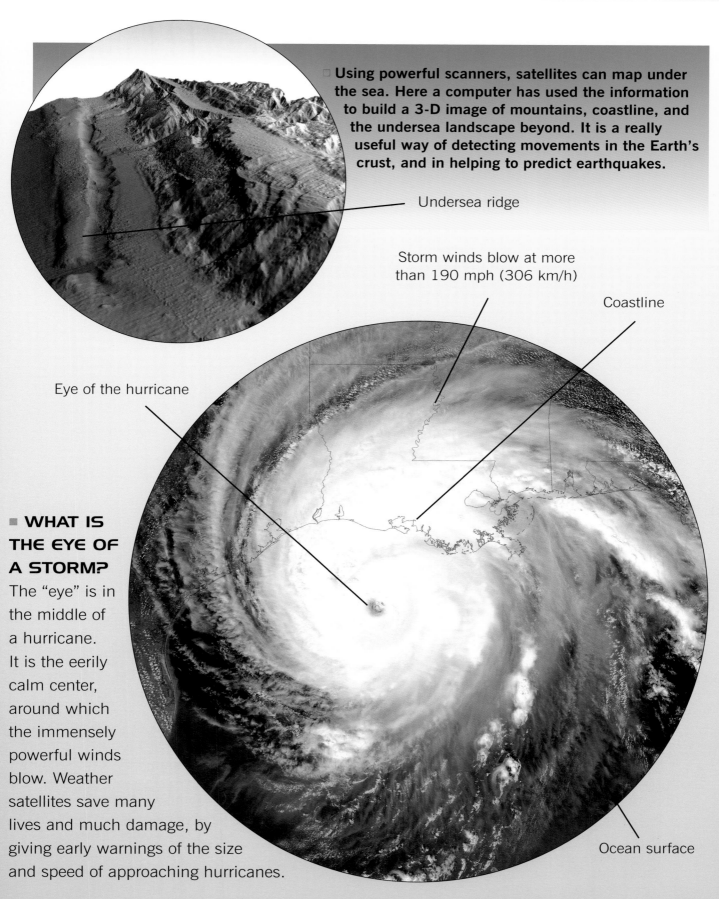

Using powerful scanners, satellites can map under the sea. Here a computer has used the information to build a 3-D image of mountains, coastline, and the undersea landscape beyond. It is a really useful way of detecting movements in the Earth's crust, and in helping to predict earthquakes.

Undersea ridge

Storm winds blow at more than 190 mph (306 km/h)

Coastline

Eye of the hurricane

■ WHAT IS THE EYE OF A STORM?

The "eye" is in the middle of a hurricane. It is the eerily calm center, around which the immensely powerful winds blow. Weather satellites save many lives and much damage, by giving early warnings of the size and speed of approaching hurricanes.

Ocean surface

■ FACTS AND FIGURES

■ EARTH STATISTICS

Diameter

The Earth bulges slightly across the middle. At the equator, it measures 7,927 miles (12,756 km) across, but from north to south it is just 7,900 miles (12,714 km).

Time to rotate

Twenty-four hours, or to be precise, 86,400 seconds. This also means that you are travelling around with the planet as it spins on its axis. At the equator you are moving with the Earth at 1,038 mph (1,670 km/h), but at the North or South Pole, you would simply be rotating on the spot.

Distance to the Sun

93 million miles (150 million kilometers) average.

Composition

The Earth's crust is made up of 47 percent oxygen, 28 percent silicon, eight percent aluminum and five percent iron. Other minerals include calcium, sodium, potassium, and magnesium.

Temperature

The Earth's surface temperature varies from day to night, season to season, and tropics to poles. The average temperature is 57°F (14°C), with a highest recorded daytime temperature of 136°F (57.7°C), and a low of -128°F (-89°C).

Surface gravity

Here on Earth we live under a force of one **gravity**, also called 1G.

☐ **This picture of the Amundsen-Scott research base in Antarctica also shows the Aurora Australis, glowing as a hazy green glow in the sky.**

The main buildings of the base (far left) are specially designed so that snow blows under them. This way, the base does not get buried!

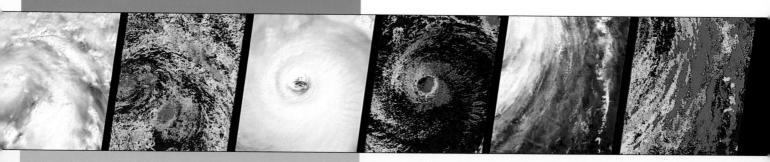

■ Earth Resources Satellites often use scanners that can observe the same view through different filters.

These can show up different parts of the object under study, such as the hurricane shown above. For example, a visible-light camera shows what it looks like to our eyes. An infrared filter shows temperatures, while other equipment can see through the cloud to record what is going on underneath.

■ FASCINATING FACTS

IS THE HUMAN POPULATION OF THE EARTH INCREASING?

Yes it is, and the ever greater numbers of people make controlling pollution and global warming more difficult. In 1950, there were about 2.5 billion people in the world. In 2000, there were 6.5 billion, and by 2050, there are likely to be some nine billion people. After that, experts think that numbers will level off, or even start to fall a little.

ARE THERE UNKNOWN PLACES YET TO BE DISCOVERED?

Almost all of the land has been explored, but the deep oceans are still largely uncharted. Up to 95 percent of the ocean floors have not yet been mapped in detail.

HOW LONG WILL PLANET EARTH SURVIVE?

Most experts think that the Earth has about five or six billion years left, before the Sun swells up to become a huge "Red Giant." It will then boil away the oceans and the air, turning the Earth into a scorched cinder.

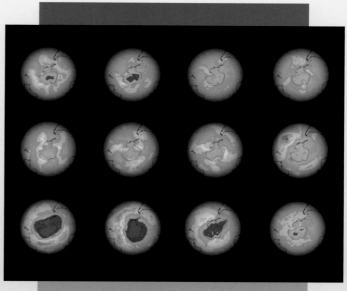

▢ In the 1970s, researchers found that polluting gases, called CFCs, were destroying the ozone layer in places, forming an "ozone hole," shown in purple and blue in the month-by-month pictures above. Reducing the use of CFCs has started to repair the damage and the ozone layer may be healed.

■GLOSSARY

Here are explanations for many of the terms used in this book.

Aphelion The nearest point of the Earth in its orbit around the Sun. The furthest point is called the perihelion.

□ **Most of the world's weather happens in the lower parts of the atmosphere.**

Atmosphere The layers of air surrounding the Earth.

Aurora A glow in the sky caused by particles from the Sun hitting the Earth's magnetic field.

Axis Imaginary line between the poles, around which the Earth rotates at an angle of 23.5 degrees.

Biosphere The parts of the Earth that are inhabited by living things.

Core The center of the Earth, thought to be made of hot, molten iron.

Crust The outermost layer of rock of a planet such as the Earth. Also called the lithosphere.

Desert A dry, barren area of land. Can be hot (such as the Sahara) or cold (such as Antarctica).

Earthquake A sudden and violent shaking of the ground, caused by movements in the Earth's crust.

Equator Imaginary line around the Earth's middle, dividing the world into northern and southern halves.

Equinox, solstice Quarterly points in the Earth's orbit around the Sun, occurring in mid-winter, mid-spring, mid-summer, and mid-fall.

Gravity The universal force of attraction between all objects.

Greenhouse effect The trapping of heat in a planet's atmosphere. Gases from pollution seem to be boosting the Earth's natural greenhouse effect, to create unwanted global warming.

Hydrosphere The seas and oceans.

Magma Hot, fluid rock from within the crust and mantle, from which lava is formed as it cools.

Magnetosphere The magnetic region around the Earth.

Mantle The molten part of the Earth between the core and the crust.

Mass The amount of matter that an object contains.

Orbit The curving path a space object takes around a more massive one, such as the Earth orbiting the Sun.

☐ Mauna Kea is a volcano whose summit forms one of the Hawaiian islands. At the top of Mauna Kea is an observatory (below), where the clear skies allow good astronomical observations.

Organism An individual living thing.

Plate A rigid piece of the Earth's crust that floats on the mantle.

Pole One of the two opposite ends of the Earth, the North and South poles.

Satellite This can be a natural object, such as the Moon, or an artificial one, such as an Earth Resources Satellite.

Seamount An underwater mountain, more than 3,280 ft (1,000 m) high.

Solar system Name for the Sun and the space objects that circle it, including the eight major planets.

Solar wind The stream of particles blowing across space from the Sun.

Subduction The sinking movement of a plate edge, down into the mantle.

Tsunami A tidal wave caused by an undersea earthquake.

Volcano A mountain or hill through which lava, rocks, vapor, and gases have erupted from the mantle.

Year The time it takes for the Earth to complete a single orbit around the Sun (a total of 365.25 days).

■ **GOING FURTHER**

Using the Internet is a great way to expand your knowledge of the Earth.

Your first visit should be to the site of the U.S. space agency, NASA. Its site shows almost everything to do with space, from the history of spaceflight to astronomy and a lot of Earth resources information.

There are also websites that give daily news on space and the planets. Try these sites to start with:

http://www.nasa.gov	A huge site.
http://landsat.gsfc.nasa.gov	Earth resources info.
http://www.terradaily.com	Interesting news site.
http://oceanexplorer.noaa.gov	Looking at the seas.
http://www.google.com/space	A night sky viewer.

■INDEX